Poems of the Two Worlds

POEMS

OF THE TWO WORLDS

Frederick Morgan

UNIVERSITY OF ILLINOIS PRESS

Urbana Chicago London

Grateful acknowledgment is made to the following magazines in which most of the poems in this book were first published: *The New Yorker:* "1949," "Exotica," "The Rescue"; *The New Republic:* "When it rained and rained," "Legend," "The Old Days," "Aubade," "Lao-Tzu," "The Step," "Question"; *The Nation:* "In Silence," "Two Cubist Poems," "Sigils," "The Circle," "The Key," "Pirate Poem," "The Exiles"; *The American Scholar:* "In a five-minute stillness in September," "Moment," "Anger at my heart one April morning"; *Commonweal:* "Maitreya," "The Puppets"; *The Hudson Review:* "Blue Hill Poems," "Autobiographies"; *The Southern Review:* "The green men march . . .," "The worm beneath the grass . . .," "Shadows," "I love grim Autumn days," "The Depths," "Winter Poem," "Umbrella Poem," "May 1, 1974"; *Kayak:* "Memories, 1 and 2," "Poems of the Two Worlds" (in an earlier version); *Michigan Quarterly Review:* "The Past," "The Letter," "Saying," "Being, I," "The devil demands perfection," "Being, II"; *The Sewanee Review:* "Memories, 3" (in an earlier version), "From a Diary, 2" (in an earlier version), "Bianca," "The Closed House," "The Gate," "Prayer"; *Poetry Now:* "The Word," "Centaurs," "Deborah Poem"; *The Georgia Review:* "The Door," "Shame," "Prisoner"; *The Paris Review:* "Elves," "Pterodactyls," "Nightwatchers"; *The Ontario Review:* "From a Diary, 1," "The Aristocrats," "Princess Poem"; *The Texas Quarterly:* "Mirrors of Childhood," "Two Poems to a Dead Woman"; *The Yale Review:* "Poem of the Gold Coin," "Body Song"; *The American Pen:* "Thaw," "Pharaoh," "Justice"; *Poetry Northwest:* "From a Forgotten Book," "Cold Poem"; *The New York Review of Books; Encounter; The Atlantic Monthly; The Columbia Forum; The Massachusetts Review; The Antioch Review; The Virginia Quarterly Review; Salmagundi; New Letters; The Malahat Review; Prairie Schooner; Poetry Nation; American Poetry Review; America; New York Arts Journal; Ploughshares.*

"Umbrella Poem" was privately printed at The Book Arts Press, December 1973, in a special edition of 50 copies designed, set in type, and printed by Paula Deitz. "From the Kuan-Tzu" was published by The Pomegranate Press, July 1974, in a special broadside edition of 180 copies. "The Walk" was published by Rook Press, April 1976, in a special broadside edition of 250 copies. "Animula" was published by The Bellevue Press, June 1976, in a limited postcard edition of 500 copies.

For Paula again

Contents

EIGHT

"At the gate of the worlds stands Truth,
and speaks a question into the world."

ONE

In Silence

Patient things wait in nature,
having undertaken to be only what they are.

Crystals bedded in gneiss,
coral undersea,
robin eggs blue in the nest. . .

"I may love you" (I hear a voice whisper)
"but remain silent—
never come looking.

'You' may have to find 'me.' "

Mirrors of Childhood

1

A small boy is moving along a country road at night. He walks
alongside stone walls feeling their roughness intimately.
Trees are very dark. Sometimes their branches lurch in the
   wind.
They're over him and looking down. Somewhere within the
   birds sleep. . .

Beyond the wall is a huge lawn: high oaks and drooping wil-
   lows
and far back, a house of stone sleeping with all its eyes dark.
Miles away, a dog barks. The wind moves through the trees
   again.
The boy goes slowly, sensing turf dense and springy beneath
   his shoes.

The wall corners away: there's a ruggedness of thickets now,
twigs and cobwebs at his face and barksmell overarching
   him—then
something makes him leave the road and thrust into the tan-
   gled brush.

He scrambles through the rough growth and up a slope in a
   small rush
releasing him to openness whereon dim grasses vaguely stir.
All about is meadow-scent, beneath a vast sky brimmed with
   stars.

2

An ogre lived in the corner wood.
His property was clearly marked.
He could not move beyond those bounds
but whoso entered them he slew.

A witch dwelt at the forest's heart
in a small hut whose chimney smoked.

She moved through the dark glades alone
and those she met she turned to stone.

Dangerous, they: if you were a fool.
Not evil, for they were contained
within their old inheritance
wherein they held acknowledged rights.

A road wound in and through their realms,
the freest road in all the world,
for those who walk it know no fear
and birds and beasts come speak to them.

3

I was held prisoner once outside of time
in a place so fair I thought I must be free.
The lawns were green, the gardens glowed with gems,
but the torturer was never far from me.

He had the key to the small door in the wall
and brought his darkness through it when he wished
and laid his claw on me, chilling my heart
until I feared I had not long to last.

Yet I was fed and cared for, and felt shame,
and gave obedience to those spirits all
until one day I found the quiet place,
the summerhouse where sings the unkempt soul.

The angled peony beds, the polished pool
burned dully in their devilled ecstasy
but I had heard the song that broke the spell,
restoring me to change and destiny.

A dampish splattering of rain shook down.
I felt my darkness bringing me to birth.
I left the garden then, and—pledged to time—
became at one with all the things of earth.

4

Sometimes I wandered to pine groves
"standing full-rigged like ships at sea,"
spoke there to my animula
who shimmered as she played with me.

Female, but not for loving, she
was like a sister or a twin,
thin and unformed with straight blonde hair
that tangled in the shifting wind:

a twelve-year-old with buds for breasts
and clear, impassive look that gave
the challenge of the changing self.
Naked, we might dance in the waves

or naked, clasp on forest floor
while sunlight sifted through pine boughs—
but what there was of intercourse
could be but what one self allows. . .

Strange Being, of my past a part,
where dance you now in your delight?
Or are we joined perhaps—so close,
you write these words even as I write?

"When it rained and rained"

When it rained and rained
and I was a child
I looked from the windows
of "39"
across the slick street and
over the roofs
of three-storey houses—
brick and white trim—
hushed in the wetness
while high in the distance
above dim facades
water-towers loomed. . .

until the front door
three flights below
slammed, and my father's voice
rhythmic, searching
rose up the stairwell
calling a name,
the name that was mine—

and I cried out too
naming him back
in our secret tongue
and ran down the deep
stairway to find him:
we met at the heart
of the darkening house

as evening set in. . . Soon
the lights would go on.

Poem of the Gold Coin

A boy in a New York room looking at the snow
that drifts down persistently outside the window panes
has closed the door to his room: he moves things about—
games, pencils, books—from desktop to bookcase to floor,
then puts those things back in their places again.
The snow still falls. Nothing in the world has changed.
His desk is painted blue and has twelve cubbyholes
in which are lodged erasers, marbles, and a small
orange-sack filled with worn old Roman coins.
In a corner are stacked frayed piles of pulp magazines.

. . . A boy in Philadelphia looking at the rain
that spills down chillingly outside the window panes
runs from his room and up back stairs to the attic
where he opens black rusting trunks and finds old silks,
daguerreotypes, disguises, daggers and
lastly, in the corner of an old brown burlap bag
a single coin—of gold. Spins it in the air!

—All changes then, accelerates—rain, snow,
New York, Philadelphia in alternation
as images of two boys shift, flickering,
and merge at times in a third who is everywhere.

Who is to tell which is real? (If either is.)
Or has each one, perhaps, made up the other?
Or must "I" come to tell it as it were my story?
If so, dark reader, "you" must imagine me.

Another change; and all is still and silent.
Empty fields extend along the shore
on which an empty ocean keeps on breaking. . .
No man nor boy nor beast—at most a bird or two:
space where the mind may seize its vaster being.

Two Cubist Poems

1

Laundry smells, kitchen smells
           a green glade in Ireland

steep stairs climbing
           a small house lingers over the hill

darkness falls with meaning
           sun rises in Ireland

black books queerly crouched
           someone waits at the top of the hill

books change to necromancers
           lie in shade in moist grass

black hats, black cloaks
           cloud-puffs in early sky

house becomes no-house
           lie in grass, let the wind blow

darkness rising into moon
           wind blow over your nakedness

what child is crying there?
           mind at ease beyond the sky

how unspeakable those longings!
           stillness and the skyward gaze

die once more into your sleep
           green glade sunning

sleep revolving into day
           mind and mind rejoining

2

Walls of glass
                furtive spirits, red blue green
whiteness bespeaks order
                green shrubs washed by rain
whiteness of patterned squares
                shrubs twisting in the wind
"I" sit. . . "I" think
                outer reflecting inner
body fastens what it may
                eyes assert the frame
transparencies within the mind
                meanings know no fixed abode
whiteness all the way within
                (outside, dark and light revolving)
angels in the whiteness, witches and ogres in the whiteness
                raindrops on the swaying shrubs
mind makes: makes or takes
                moment undoes time
within crystal = mirror
                gray cat creeping along the fence top
subdue your colors, eidolon
                gray cat leaps down from the fence
transparent behind walls of glass
                green of day, ungreen of night
whose mind is?
                cool shrubs bending in the rain
body does, again does
                something is. In the rain

The Past

Wind from the frozen lake
in black New Hampshire night
froze the tears to my face.

It was 1936,
deep winter—as I ran
under an aching moon
(quite at the end of my tether)

back to the graceless halls
of that forbidding school
where stunted men had rule
over young growing lives.

I spoke to my weeping heart:
"Freeze now and be still—
impassive as this glass—
then, feel pain no more."

Poor heart obeyed, congealed;
I held it hard within
and thus we two survived.

But I would pay a price
for having a heart turned ice:
years and years must pass
before I loved at last.

Memories

1

A showery summer afternoon: the leaves
dripped softly as I walked down the drenched path
home from a friend's. I liked the touch of rain,

fresh drops shivering down my back as I brushed
through the corner hedge and crossed the lawn to our house.
I ran in, soaking: had the place to myself, I thought.

Up in my room I was naked, drying off
when I saw you standing at the open door—
I ducked down, clutching the towel. "Don't be afraid," you
    said,

"don't hide from me" (I was crouched down by the bed)
"your parents have gone out. We're alone here now."
You came to me, touched my face. I slowly stood up.

You were Swedish: worked for us as chambermaid.
I remember your eyes, chestnut with amber flaws,
your skin, your mouth—much else besides. . .

Months later, in time of war, you left our house,
married a man with a Slavic name and started
a home of your own. You came calling once:

buxom, neat, in sleek department-store dress,
your hair in a "permanent wave," you talked to my mother
respectfully commonplace over cups of tea

and when I entered, smiled and shook my hand
and said, "How well you're looking! How is college?"
—while I thought back on that long day of rain

and the fierce freshness of your body's touch.

2

After the opera
night of fog
we went back to your rooms
cooked bacon and eggs

I took off my jacket
you, your long gown
big girl that you were
I was strongly drawn

by rampish plump breasts
held tense in the bra,
I soon set them loose
(you laughing the while)

and licked those large nipples—
we went on from there
to bedroom and bed
there was much to explore

long peaceful billows
of buttock and bust
I was holding a goddess
giantess, beast

in my arms—so it seemed
as you panted and heaved
and when we got going
I was riding huge waves

I was deep in old Egypt
I was fucking a cow!
We yelled and collapsed
flopped down any-old-how

pulled up the mussed covers
and slept until dawn

your slow-breathing body
heavy by mine . . .

When I left, in the chill
of a day just begun,
you reached a big arm out,
said, "Thanks, it was fun."

3

Greenness of spring leaves on
Friday the 13th of
April, where I walked
in Central Park, in coolness.

Sun on my back hinted
its summer fullness
as a light breeze glanced off
the reservoir's face.

A boy in gray sweat-clothes
jogged past sturdily
frayed sneakers splashing
the cinder track—

trucks dumped their dirt at
a black asphalt siding,
a horse-girl cantered by
blonde, straight-backed—

sparrows took their dust-baths
beneath the pale-green bushes,
mothers trundled baby-carts
past soiled children playing tag—

as quietly, the primal
fresh smell of water
eased in where my heart was clenched
upon a love long lost.

The Door

for Robert Penn Warren

Stranded late at night when the blackout came
I found I didn't know that city well.
It seemed the streets were all alike:
row after row of blank-faced houses
bulky in the gloom of their high front stoops.

I looked for a main way leading downtown
but kept getting nowhere, or back where I started.
A helmeted warden yelled me to shelter—
soon the bombers would be coming over.

Moon almost full. I paused halfway down
a street like the others with no numbers on the houses
and leaned against a wall in a blotch of darkness.
Somewhere nearby cabbage was cooking,
from an unseen yard a dog yelped twice.

Then—shuffling sounds from close above me
and an old voice gasping, "Rachel! Where are you?"—
gasping and choking, "Oh my God, what have they done to
    you?"

I chilled inside. Looked up and saw
a dark door opening on emptier darkness
and an old man, stringy-necked, standing and swaying:
he wore a brown robe, his mouth was twisted.

"Is there trouble?" I asked, and went up two steps.
His blurred face blinked, but made no answer.
Across the way a window opened.
"You had best go back in," I said, "there's going to be
    danger."

"Danger," he moaned—then came words I made no sense of,
and "God God God—the danger's in *there!*"
He turned, pointing, then rushed at the blackness

15

and vanished, as though he'd been gulped into nothing.
The door closed, all was quiet again.

The bombers didn't come. Alone with the moon
I wandered those empty streets for hours
and when at long last I found the surly warden
there was really nothing at all that could be done.
The houses, the doors were all the same.

The Letter

He mailed that letter many years ago—
the friend I knew in early army days—
from Germany in 1946.
(He'd stayed on in the service, "marking time.")

It came to my old post after I'd gone,
was forwarded from there to the wrong man
(who strangely had my name) at some remote
specialist-battalion in the mountains,

then—missent once again—crossed the Pacific
and following me where I had never been
moved from one jungle depot to another:
at some it lingered months or even years

before being sent along its stumbling way
at last, with one more wrinkle on its brow.
Old, frayed, and black with changes, it arrived
last night—and brought me good news of myself.

1949

.

1

Under the arbor
          Renée
in your red-and-white-striped shirt
you don't mind
          do you
if I kiss you?

Two or three birds
          in a small flurry
rise to the other world at the tops of the trees—
I like your lips
          (warm, red)
and the hoops that dangle golden from your ears.

2

Come on in, Griselda,
          the water's fine,
black mud bottom
          OK when you get used to it
and no bloodsuckers—
          not in this old pond.

Hovering at the center, I
          can look up at the sky's
pale circle rimmed with tree-tops:
          come on in, Gris,
let your big breasts float
          free on the dark water,

I want to see them swaying
          and all that red hair too
in the three o'clockish sun
          as you come
splashing in. We'll
          see the shadows later.

18

From a Diary

1

At the end of the street the ocean
breathes out its intricate mumblings
to a huge beach emptied by war.

Days of sun. Bicycling, reading—
Thérèse Desqueyroux on hot sand.
Coconuts afloat by the lake-shore
in shade of torsed palms leaning out.

At evening, from the Spanish-style villa
a piano's cool ripplings: Fauré.
A flaxen-haired girl, enigmatic,
stands by the patio gate.

Cocktails. Cut-outs of palm fronds
black in the incredible moon.
Night-smell of hibiscus—and the hot embrace
of this woman I have not known.

Unutterable the suavity,
the loss, and impassioned waste.
On New Year's eve a drunkard howls
down our hotel's long dim arcades.

Palm Beach, 1942

2

Sunset: the mists move in from ocean inlets
across rough stands of salty brush.
An island's images are dimmed
within the moment's cool equivocations.

Glass of whiskey in hand
I pause in the dusk outside the kitchen door
feeling at my face the chill excitement
of channel foam blown damply in.

Wife, children, books, a dog, a rented house—
the daily furnishings—
retain but tentative existence in
this pale continuum of mist and spirit,

as though one's self had still to cleave itself
from time's residuals
into its final truth: a shape
bright and unclouded, even though unseen.

Over the moors the mists are gathering,
the sparse fields fade
but heart—sequestered—thrills, as from within
dark Eros calls me onward through the years.

Nantucket, 1947

3

North of 96th where the tracks come out from under
the sun brightens on morning pavements,
the tired air begins to stir.

Puerto Rican streets in Sunday stillness.
An old fat sofa, guts spilling out,
suns itself on the soiled sidewalk.

From a low doorway deep in soot
a child peers, agate-eyed—
a stray dog lopes along, waving his frazzled tail.

The breeze blows grit into my eyes
as I pass a vacant lot girt with rotting fence-boards.
Stevenson's face looks out from tattered posters
alert and fatigued, somehow beyond it all.
"We must look forward to great tomorrows."

Over on Lexington the bars are closed,
the pawnshops gated tight—but the corner luncheonette,
where you can get the greasiest fried eggs in town,
is doing good business with its counters jammed.

A skinny girl passing by gives me the eye,
I smile and look down. A newspaper blows past.

Down the street a nun—thin, white-faced—
gathers her children about her: but now they're on top of me
in a scraggly column, running and shoving their way
toward the parish school of St. Francis de Sales.
The nun's face is lined, mouth down-drawn, but from the eyes
something fragile glints that may be happiness.

Or so I propose—as I wonder why it all
happens the way it happens, and what will befall
myself and the world, as time runs out—

and tell myself at last to be still and not mind.
Today, held firm, is my tomorrow.

New York, 1953

Exotica

1
White gown transparent on her,
"torse and limb shone through"
           (in winter, in New York, in '42)—
outside, a few lights in the dark apartments.

2
Her body by candlelight had that elegant look—

           but eyes were bruised and "tragic,"
the house half-shrouded for a winter of war,
the letter—shrivelled like a stricken moth. . .

3
Bought girl, braceleted Arab, Zayn-al-Mawasif,
dance! as prelude to the hungry night.

4
Her spirit moved towards me across the harbor,
over the water it moved like a shadow of light.

Spirit is tenuous. *She* was far away.
The air moved damply to the foghorn's groaning.

5
Too late. . .
rain. . .

That bitch Mathilde takes on another man.

6
Who used to read to me of Eloisa's love
in the park, late afternoons, by lake of swans. . .
who with white weak hands,
turning the pages in a whiter sadness?

7
Touch me not with gauzy hair
          or skimmering nipple,
ephemerid!

8
Steeped in the cunt
my deep descent—

freedom beyond what's human.

9
Russet-brown, copper-pink
bold-blotched with black and sinewy—
mute spirit of the brushlands,
Surucucu the quick-striking.

10
Anteaters
in dreams
were a horror to Alexandra. . .

11
Misunderstanding on the plane to Cairo!
Carlotta went to sulk beside the Sphinx
          while I—immaculate, estranged—
turned my thoughts to the endless plains of Kenya.

12
Lizard in the sunshine,
lemur under the moon,
she fled the city of
my ten thousand faces.

13
Paris. The hotel. The morning after.
I felt remote from the sound of Ellen's laughter.

Wanted to get at the news in the morning papers—
more or less indifferent to last night's capers.

14
Blue-lashed
in the smoky moon,
Aissa. . .
                    (phony Arab name!)
Fucking me for francs near the docks at Cherbourg.

15
La Malbaie: in the herb-garden by twilight
at summer's end I caught the "swift Camilla":
we rode each other through the purple night.

16
Never forget. The cool and gritty wind
over the New York streets those early winter
mornings of the 1930's, when
I looked out from my window all alone. . .

TWO

Sigils

1
I was released
               as butterfly
from lip of the bright cup

2
I grew
downward
through dense roots
into the heart
of metal

3
I poured myself
like water
    diminishing
             into sand

4
I crumbled
         but my touch
remains
hard on the polished stone

5
. . . Caterpillar,
            from blade to blade
I moved—from life
         to life

The Circle

Snakefish, *anguilla*,
spend greater part of life in ponds and streams
but "on the approach of sexual maturity"
pass down to the sea:

under the west Atlantic, halfway
between Bermuda and the Leeward Isles
at 3000 fathoms' depth
spawn, then die.

From the eggs *leptocephali*—
tiny, transparent, willow-leaf shaped—
emerge and grow, at last migrate
to the upper water layers
and swim back to America.
It takes two years.

Three years old, they change to elvers,
ascend the rivers in the spring
and make their way inland in millions
wriggling across damp fields at night
into the smaller lakes and streams.

Here they live ten years or twenty,
their growth "determined by the food supply"
until the inner urge compels them
down, once more, into the sea.

The Key

Come unto the
yellow sands
where shells of gastropods abound:

the hermits here
hide their soft
abdomens in the homes they've found

and in their thousands
purple-clawed
climb trees to feed on mangrove sap.

Many other
arthropods
occupy this habitat

but only roaches
(it appears)
compete with them for food—

both tribes swarm up
the woven roots
in search of juice which they find good

but neither pays
the other mind:
a taciturn neutrality

prevails among
the armored throngs
of equal creatures. Similarly

black widow spiders
scorpions
earwigs, orb weavers, dragonflies

may all inhabit
one small beach
without occasioning surprise.

It's as it were a
unity
of strangers going separate ways

within a shared
environment
which none has power to rule or change.

Whale Poem

All of the bones of five toes are in each of his paddles
and under the blubber the bones of unused hind legs.

The tail (unlike a fish's, horizontal)
is rudder and propeller both, and drives him
with strength of seventy horses abruptly down
hundreds of feet to depths at which his body
must bear many tons of pressure per square inch.

Rising, he may release the used-up breath
just before reaching the surface: at such times
a mixture of water and breath blows up from the sea.

I read about him first in Kipling's story—how
the sailor he swallowed foxed him by blocking his throat—
but the truth about the baleen whale was more surprising.
His mouth is a maze. He has no teeth.
Enormous plates of horn in the upper jaw,
frayed at the edges as though rough-combed for use,
lie flat, toward the throat, when the mouth is closed—
when it opens, they are raised and hang down like fringed
    curtains.
As he swims through the sea open-mouthed, a living cavern,
thousands of little life-forms are trapped in the fringes;
when the mouth closes, the water strains out at the sides
but these remain and fall down on the tongue to be swal-
    lowed.
(They have to be small—his throat couldn't take in a herring!)

A sperm whale, on the other hand, can swallow a Jonah
or something still larger. His mouth takes up one third
the length of a body that may extend sixty feet.
The sperm oil lies in a cavity alongside his head
and ambergris—used as fixative in making perfumes—
may, when he's in poor health, form in his guts.
It used to be found in great masses, floating on southern seas.

The whale I saw in '49 or '50
was a smaller kind, maybe a grampus—I'd say
about twenty-five feet. He surfaced off our boat
(Eddie Sherman's lobster-boat, which Dr. Moorhead
had chartered for his annual fishing trip:
we had our lines out, anchored in the mouth of Blue Hill Bay)
one hundred yards out to sea, and blew and spouted—
a hollow whistling more vibration than sound—
then sank, and surfaced once more about ten minutes later
on our other side, a little bit closer—and we laughed.
We got the message: greatness, freedom, and ease.

They're mammals; the mothers nurse their young.
We hunt them, sink our barbs into their flesh—
using explosives now in our harpoons—
hoist the vast bleeding bodies to the decks
of "factory ships," where the live flesh is rent from the bone.
They may have thoughts in their heads: we do not know.

Sometimes I think of the great sum of pain
endured by inoffensive giant bodies
torn, ripped, chopped, dismembered in their millions
by the sharp tricks of a smart race of maggots.
Is there justice in the universe? We'd better hope not.

I had a dream once, in which I was swallowed by a whale
and thought it was the end and something horrible—
but it all opened up, like the Mammoth Cave,
in long strange hallways—stalactites, stalagmites gleaming—
and light in the distance where someone was waiting for me.

They may have thoughts—we do not know. But far
beneath the surface, where a few still live and play,
they summon each other in high-pitched signalings
and sing deep day-long songs we'll never learn.

32

Blue Hill Poems

1

The green men march along the ground
into the thickets without sound
then swarming forth, they march once more
where the cool grasses edge the shore.

Half-stillness . . . and translucent mutter—
light skirmishings of wind and water—
in glimmering thousands at midday
blue Christs are striding on the bay.

2

We have acquaintances
            up at the quarry:
a lettuce-green frog balances in the shaded corner
nose and eyes peering up from the shallows,
a water-boatman with scarlet head
glides along the watertop (he doesn't like my feet),
dragonflies in tandem hover and glisten,
a chipping sparrow rustles in the low laurel-bush
—there he goes with his *click click click*

as in the great midst we swim alone,
            naked and serene.

3

Do not wait for the owl to come out
before you play your games.

The owl sleeps in the tree all day,
at night he comes out to hunt and hoot.

He sleeps in the old weary pine-tree
but at night his eyes are whirlpools

33

and when he flies over the house his shadow
carries the house with it above the pines

to a shining lonely place where calm eyes watch
in the moonlight—but our eyes are always closed.

4

At the tide-pool pocketed in broken granite
lives converge.
A gull skims over; flies hum
and circle, settle on the scummed salt surface.
I lie on the rocks as flat as I am able
eyes focused on the small world
as a bee gleams by, lazingly.
Beneath, in sedimented green
a white-purple starfish curls,
his inner tendrils moving delicately,
and a crab size of my thumb
pale-green as a young apple
scuttles under green-brown seaweed
with a clean movement of legs.

The sun bakes my back,
granite edges dint my thighs,

I raise my head. Out and beyond
the silly sailboats skimmer on the bay
(summer sailors at their Saturday races)
and the sun is high and gold and somewhere else,
somewhere where life is rare—
it's as though, in the deep day's expanded gaze,
you were extracted from the physical
into a realization beyond what you knew:

Who speaks to me of the Person in the sun—
in annihilation's blaze the one who sings?

Here, though, at my center of things
where the heat is intimate, intense
I'm pressed down hard into my own self-knowledge
and the world of private understandings:
no vision but one's own
as rock and weed endure
and the stubborn crab maintains a brief existence
becoming a part of self and self's perception
(time drawing still and holding
steady in this clear light).
"What is small survives," I speak the words
remembering how it all in time will end—
"what is small prevails."
I say it to the sun and to myself.

5

To Paula

The worm beneath the grass
tingles against moist roots,
the yellow-jacket drills
deep into pulpy fruit—
it is a pale gold day
with ripplings in the air:
I take your hand, dear girl—
at once am everywhere.

6

Nothing is better than seaweed on rocks
and barnacles that scrape
and the harsh rub of granite
and the wind from the south bringing salt

except the sight of you naked—
everlasting love—
arms lifted, balancing lightly
as you enter the naked wave.

7

(North Sedgwick)

In the deep afternoon
            August shade
at the edge of shimmering
            asphalt, three
Indian children are sitting.

Micmacs from Canada
            down for the
blueberries, they have brilliant
            muskrat eyes,
inquiring feminine faces.

In a moment we have
            driven past,
retaining though the imprint:
            T-shirts' pale
lavender, deep blue dungarees.

8

Eyes looked at me from the old stone wall
down among roots at the bay's edge.
I said, "Eyes—believe I am not here at all
but only a spirit passes by
and you can't see spirits or know what they are
beyond these quiverings of salty air
as you reach from your lurking-place of leaves and pebbles
across the granite ledge."

Time and place made no reply.
The eyes awaited no command.
There was nothing, perhaps, to understand
in all that glowing sun-drenched sky
and wave-sheet mirroring in to land.

Eyes looked on eyes, being self-imbued,
then those eyes faded and mine turning away
to distant borders of the resplendent day
released themselves from the doubled view,
diminishing to simple spheres—
intelligent, contained—that could
describe the circle of one only world
bedazzling in its solitude:

and wave, and boat, and bird were silent
crystallizations of a mind
seeking the union known by sense
when senses give back from their strivings
into the brightness that is blind.

Eyes then denote a center of being
with radius of sense and comprehension
and what the being is, the eyes don't know,
unapt to turn back on themselves
or look behind. Being is known only
by being itself, in its own dimension—
yes, eyes are holes in the world's face, through which some-
    thing else
does its own huge seeing.

9

Cricket in the kitchen,
    you hum a pleasing song
as I fix myself a pineapple and rum:

I may not care to see you
    but I like your self-assertion.
To your health, then—little bird of the end of summer.

10

Oh, unapproachable One,
whom yet through this night of soft rain
I feel coolly stir at my heart,

through all my deaths and my lives
may I flow in your presence, and sing—
as I follow the shapes of my selves—
your glory, your peace, your abundance.

11

October in Maine. The human touch:
outboards, power saws, and guns.
A landscape fading into death endures
the idiot stutterings, fatalistically.

I listen and I think. Where might be
a true New England emptied of the human?
Forest, lake unswerving through their changes
old as the total earth, fresh as this dawn
and unwatched always but by one still man—
or man and woman, waiting quietly.

THREE

The Word

for Allen Tate

1

At dawn a word was spoken
on the glimmering shore.
A man seized it, lost it.
Death came. There were no words more

*

A child crawled out of the ocean
dragging her serpent tail.
The birds whistled on the high meadows
not apprehending the evil

*

Was I there, too—did I see it
with these or other eyes,
the lapse in time that brought eclipse of being?

*

Couplings on the uncertain land
engendered an anxious beast
who grimly grew his human head
but found no resting-place

*

The Innocence abandoned
basked on mirroring waves—
dove at last to seamless depths
not knowing her own fair face

*

Sea is drink for the mind
(so the Upanishad teaches)
and mind, drift to the wave.
Man gives meat to death
his corpse to the graveyard rats
but death is food in Me

2

I write, and the sky outside
turns violet in the evening
above the chilly waters of the bay.
I'm there, outside a body,
seeing without its seeing

*

The universe is broken into minds.
An ancient woman, dying at full moon,
holds all its memories in her one zero

as in my childhood an old French governess
walking me down Connecticut roads at evening
told me its legends, her black skirts rustling stiffly

*

How many years ago was it
I walked across another beach at night
alone and miles from home, feeling my blood
charged with the sea—saw then in pale moon-glare
along the wave that streaming primal hair
and naïve nipple rising from the foam?

*

(One may not see all that is there:
only glimpse something of the all that's not.)

*

Now, a smell of brown bread toasting
comes from the kitchen . . . I can hear
late outboards buzzing on the bay
children calling over the water—
lovely, but none of it matters
to the violet sky that darkens

42

3

The white sun sinks into the sea
the day's light dims to dark
life fails, but in the rushing wave
I feel my strength enduring

*

What voices are sounding over the water?
What child is it who calls?
The garden snake has rustled through the grass
back to his hole by the stone wall—
the tide soughs on the rocky beach
the birds have gone to nest

*

Tic toc tic toc tic toc water
tic toc tic toc tic a wave
tic toc tic toc life and death and
tic toc tic a heart amazed

*

I thought I saw a dead man walk just now
out on the point beneath the apple trees
where the mist was coming in. . .

*

And the winds are walking underground
in the second world—with a hushing sound:
familiars of earth and death
they wait for what must come to pass

*

Breathe softly: the child of dawn
approaches her midnight throne.
Remember, too,
as child I scream in my dreams

4

The incomplete uneasy Beast
with manlike grimace on his face
thrusts claws into the true man's heart
who dying breathes the word of life

*

Blood pours from the wounded side
and blood will drown the aching world—
see, from the astonished ground
a hand breaks forth that wields a sword!

*

And the strong spell is spoken.
If it kills, it kills.
Creatures of this cringing world
I speak it for your ill.
If you have no truth in you
nor loyal breath
there is no purge but in your blood
no cure but in your death

*

The violet sky is gone to black
watersounds are stilled

and time draws inward in the leaf
the wave, the mountain
joined to the ever-dying heart
by threads of green

*

Those footsteps, now, on the dark beach
crunching the bracky kelp—
must they not be my own?

5

The good man who is dead,
how may I speak his praise?
He walked the broad seashore
on the first day of days
holding his hand out to his god
beneath the sun's pure blaze

*

But now he's dead
and earth is whelmed
and none may speak the word—
trust alone
the beating wave
and the hand that wields the Sword

6

Close upon midnight, while I sleep,
far down the beach the tide turns
and a breeze lifts in from the water.

Bats circle, whisking through the pallid air

*

The nightmare comes again.
Oh God, that crawling man who hissed—
and skin of my own dear hand that turns to scale!

*

It is all one
it is all You
mind and sea and the changing worlds—
the coursing cloud
the rotting corpse
it is all you
it is all One

*

Child, as the night gains grip upon these northern shores
from the scarfed sky in bands of light
the kraken undulates his boding arms

while in my dreams a mermaid yields her charms

*

Sleep comes from the ocean
sleep moves over the land
sleep is but a breath from death
so open, now, your hand

*

Be content: for sword is sheathed
and evil head struck down.
The beast bleeds out his filth into the furrow

7

When Boreas comes hooting from the underworld
he brings us news of those we may call heroes,
persons we were, persons we're doomed to be
each holding out to us a torch or chalice,
watching us from a blackness touched with silver

*

At zero hour a thunderclap!
Then, from between the worlds
sound of the dawn wind rising

*

Let spider weave his web
before he parch to dust
man unfold his life
in patterns as he must
but free of adoration

*or clutching of the heart
holding self beyond the act
ready to depart*

*

Mornings when I awake, the sky—pale-pearl—
rests upon the bay's gray brimming waters
in silent echo of the universe

until a band of orange-pink glows up,
a gull shrieks, and the crows break out in chorus

*

Touched by the sun's mild lance
the child afloat on the freshening wave
opens her mouth to the sky

*

The mists withdraw from the damp beach.
I smell the salt, I taste the early grass

8

I write, but it is not "I"—
wave, leaf, mountain
write themselves in me.

The book of the world has opened to my page

*

Bluebirds a-wing over fields of hay:
good luck on a midsummer day!

*

The old man lies asleep in the sun
on the parched grass of summer—
he sleeps and wakes, lives or dies
at one with what he dreams

*

Time is healed, an end of toil—
blood of the beast works richly through the soil—
the mermaid, blissful, glimmers in the deep
the snake is self-consumed in sleep

*

Stones. . .
birds. . .
silence. . .
words. . .

*

Joy to the fellows of my heart,
persons of woodland, of shore and sea—
joy to the brethren of my heart
dwelling in magnanimity

*

What is the word the wind knows?
I'll speak it, once, in my life
before my body goes down under the ground

FOUR

From a Forgotten Book

When we stormed the city Sirk in the mountains
we put to the sword that foul, misshapen people:
cut down men, women, children where they stood.
Their corpses choked the streets, dogs drank their blood.

Four hundred of us slaughtered forty thousand
joyously, for we did not like their smell.
We gave ourselves to war as to a goddess;
each time we struck we struck to kill.

Spirits of our fathers woke in us
dooming to hell that stinking maggot-swarm
of soft manipulators, puny cheats
who held the honor of the brave in scorn.

I found my destined one: small, sly and fat,
leaving behind a spoor of squirrel slime
he turned, hyena-faced, to bare his teeth
and giggle, as I struck him the last time.

Our fathers know us. Violent and true
followers of the ultimate great Khan
foredoomed to dwindle down the stony years,
we've eaten death but never tasted fear.

I took my red-haired sister to my bed
that night, for each had killed a hundred men,
and felt her savage body leap with mine.
Then like two wolves replenished in their den

austere in furs beneath our snowy tent
we sucked the mountain air chill under stars—
our minds appeased, our bodies deeply spent,
while absence glittered in our perfect hearts.

Centaurs

Centaurs' habits are not of the nicest.
At parties they'll get drunk and start to fight
and smash the furniture—what's more, they're certain
to put their hands on every woman in sight.

They sprout such huge erections it's unnerving
(their throbbing members swell to sapling size)—
then as if proud of these uncouth protrusions,
rearing, they'll challenge you to feast your eyes.

Once in this state, of course, they'll stick it into
woman, mare, cow—whatever has a cunt—
release the enormous flood, then pull out crudely
and canter off with no more than a grunt.

They stuff themselves at table, belch and guzzle,
shouting "More food!" when others try to talk;
right in plain view they'll raise their tails up idly,
dropping their dung where others wish to walk.

Yet—they're acknowledged wise, and the old medals
portray them noble-browed, stern-faced, serene
with full combed beards and philosophic features.
Was there a balance struck? If so, what does it mean?

We've learned of double natures and their conflicts
(the "lower" burns, the "higher" seeks control),
perhaps should look on them as localizations,
chancewise manifest, of an unbounded whole

that's humorous, irrational, impassive,
yielding no "clear ideas" to any "mind,"
graspable only as night-skies are grasped
in strength of hopeless love by those born blind:—

for cold-cast eye may not deny the sorrow
of the great surging brute below, whose lust
must find fulfillment in its each occasion
as body comes to know itself in dust.

Body Song

When body is young
senses touch joy
they are near its green boundaries
can see tree-tops waving—
burn their boats then,
dance on the beach
the air in their lungs
sharp-tinged by the sea
each day an exile into new brilliance

Still the ghost walks
this side of joy
blond at midday
over blond sand
striding and shining
repeating the legend
body once knew,
of integral pain

Senses are stilled in the fume of the surf
subdued by that chant
to the primitive hush
that held the first body
calm in the womb—
and body has aged
when the wave comes back in

Joy is forgotten
or held in soiled hands
of a body that aches
but tastes as it wills,
with mind as its servant
to bring the rich broth
of sorrow and loss
the gift of the past—
and the tree-tops still wave
where no footprints were made

Bianca

Where are you, Bianca Capello, beautiful child
whose "deadly hand has faln upon your lord"?
I knew you in my youth's uncertain years—
now in my strength I summon you again.

You overreached. . . It's purgatory, perhaps,
this being born again life after life—
in the same form or almost, with the same eyes
reflecting a deep underworld of meaning,

yes, all this beauty, all this grace renewed—
subject to fat-faced husband, yelping brats
who spoil as they grow and break your heart at last.
—If so, there is an end. . . I saw you once

behind a Tuscan albergo, looking down
a scuffed slope where your five plump pups were howling
egged on by the idiot-grinning father. God!
You had an inward look. Were you thinking of poison?

So stern your face, severe. Wind lifted your hair.
Should I have said "I love you" in Italian?
I didn't: something there not to be touched
but left in peace for long unravelings.

Just a few words then, dear, to mark your doom:
She was born near Venice and she used to love
those trees that mutter to the western sky
at evening.   The rest is still to come.

Pirate Poem

Behind the mountain's belly-button
(press it and it lets you in)
pirates hid ten chests of gold
guarded by a skeleton.

In one scanty hand he held
a sword upraised to strike you down;
the other clutched a blanching skull
the mirror-likeness of his own.

Above, on the fresh mountainside
where austral breezes stirred sparse shrubs,
couched in a higher, cooler cave
a she-bear nursed her huddled cubs.

The pirates went their several ways:
some were hanged and some were drowned
and some retired as country men,
but one returned to that far ground

twenty years later, found the navel,
pressed it—and it let him in—
stepped across the threshold, saw
by torch's light the skeleton,

who gently set down skull and sword,
stood up, stretched out imploring hands. . .
The other turned and fled. And fell—
and bleached white on the island sands.

Legend

Lonesome on the cliffside
lonesome on the prairie
twilight to twilight the
ageless American rides

long prick tucked into
sweat-shiny britches
between his thighs the on-
ward undulations of the horse

past the flat-top mesa
where a last saurian lurks
past the claptrap vistas
of dead movie sets

to where an ancient judgment
waits in the salt canyon
unlinked from all the past
which somehow passed him by

The Rescue

Around the old old islands
    old old crocodiles swim
eye-sockets like croquet wickets
    glinting in the sun.

Their wicked eyes transfix you,
    little naked man
splashing from the sea-wreck
    of the great ship *Caliban*

to those green Encantadas—
    at least, that's your idea,
despite the tricky creatures
    grinning from ear to ear.

You head for the far bull's-eye
    through circles of bright teeth—
there, at last you've made it,
    hard land beneath your feet.

You stumble through the shallows
    retching up bile and brine,
crawl across crusted ledges
    aglitter with sea-shine

and now, passing the tide-mark,
    shed weak and thankful tears. . .
Something's a little wrong, though,
    there's not much greenness here—

just black volcanic scourings
    to scorch the tender skin
and sun and rock and tortoises
    and sea-birds shrieking down

the winds that blow from elsewhere.
    Is "elsewhere" home? You've come
where there's no getting back without
    another, longer swim.

Woyzeck

Woyzeck 1:   It wasn't my woman's infidelity
             or even the visions of blood that did me in
             but the damned assurance of the educated
                ones.

Captain: I wish to be a good man, don't you know,
             but that idea—"eternity"—confuses me:
             mirrors unending!

Marie: The children lost in the fairy tale
             came to the ogre's house.
             He drew his knife—but as midnight
                struck
             they ran away through the dark dark
                forest.

Woyzeck 2:   A beard all over her body—ugh!
             lips opening, the gush of red. . .

Drum Major: A woman is a hole:
             one enjoys the going in
             but even more the climbing free again.

Fool: What I don't know is in the books.
             I know the smell of blood.

Knife: Without volition of my own
             I performed the task appointed.
             Now I must rust until the end of time.

Woyzeck 3:   Truly, the pond was what I wanted all
                along:
             the cool torpor, mud
             closing my mouth and eyes.

Doctor: Children, be glad! I know those answers.
             Soon my voice alone will be heard in the
                land.

Marie's Ghost:	Savior, savior, spare my soul! I'll wash your feet in my warm tears.
Pond:	I hold what was and will be. Reflecting the moon, I think of gold.
Child:	Dawn once more: the heavy dawn. What day is ever new?
Woyzeck's Ghost:	A long march ahead of me— back, back, past all the persons.

The Exiles

At night they moved from room to room glinting,
with under the nightdress a bangle or two
and wine at the bedside in tall decanters
in which to pledge the perilous name.

They felt they were doomed most likely, but tried
each day to deny the future, the past,
as they rode brown fields on horseback
revisiting the further farms.

Deep Autumn: tinge
of apples dusky on the air
when nights drop sharply down, and dawns
reveal quick scatterings of frost.

Letters arrived from time to time
mostly with word of deaths:
the ways of the fathers and mothers were strange
but not as strange as the chill present.

How would it end—this game, this dream—
in sudden silence all about
with black skies falling to the earth,
or by slow sequence of cessations?

The world in sum was muck, they thought,
paltry and diseased—
and if indeed a god held sway
he should have worked first on himself,

done something for his private lacks
before presuming to bring forth
other minds touched with his malaise
and dim resentment of the void.

They saw their shadows, caught in his huge mirror.

The Old Days

All the way back from the graveyard
the jazz-band played loud sweet and free—
they were earning two dollars apiece,
a hell of a lot for those days.

Along the dirt road men and boys
swung axe-handles, baseball bats, broomsticks
to drive the ghost-men away
and keep the blood moving inside them.

There'd be blood on the outside, too,
when some gang from the far end of town
paying no heed to the hex-lines
would cross where they had no damn business—

We played all our favorite hymns,
drank gin and warm whiskey and beer
and packed in fried fish and fried chicken
reminiscing about the departed.

And three or four would make speeches,
one would cry, and one tell funny stories
while the soul, rising clean from the graveyard,
fled "free as a bird to the mountain."

The Priest

Sacrificing
to the four quarters
I find the winds responsive.

The rains come
and I wish them here.
I walk without shoes in the rain.

Once from a bush a voice spoke to me—
from the old brown skull
of a murdered man:

he told me his life-story.
Hearing, I knew it once more.

And once, in the forest of Ro-ku
when I was far into silence,
a bear lived with me for a week.

When I dream, it is of the true
forests of the second world
crowded with bears and ghosts.

I was born in the northernmost island,
woodcutter's son,
lived my first twenty years
as servant to my father.

On the day that he was buried, I
went wandering through the trees—
from the pine I learned of the pine,
and of the oak from the oak.

Hideyoshi

After the last battle,
the enemy having been cut to pieces,
he rode a short distance from the field
and dismounted.

Sat in his armor on the grass
and gave word to his staff
that he wished to make a flower-arrangement—
they, however, lacked the equipment.

So he took a bucket, and his horse's bit
(which he hung by one ring from the bucket-handle)
and rigged them into a flower-holder,

then with his bloody sword
cut wild blossoms and grasses
and in an hour's silence
composed a subtle and delicate combination. . .

Those whom he had conquered
he now must judge:
he wished a mind clean-purged
of violence and ardor.

Maitreya

Life is a flame (he said)
before the wind blows. . .

life is a flame
as though in itself enduring.

Not much to be done, when all is said,
about that wind.

After a year—or
a billion years it may be,

speech to be extinguished,
the mobile body shudder to its end

and the words array themselves
on a high meadow, burning.

FIVE

Bones

The bones go under the soil, under the soil
at year's end the bones go under the soil—
sometimes they wave red flags
sometimes they speak not at all

The bones are boats that go sailing in the black ground
clean through the earth and out the other side
in an everyday kind of way
into the sun again

The bones speak to the birds, the birds sing back
but the language is lost before it comes to the ears
of fools who run to and fro
between the birds and the bones

I killed a fool once and drank blood from his skull
and taking his bony fingers in my hand
asked him where he wanted to go:
he didn't say yes, he didn't say no

Bones have a home underground or so I'm told.
They are themselves the city in which they dwell
and have a meaning, too, since they once were we:
another meaning is coming, wait and see

Grandfather Poem

Grandfather stepped out from the clock
at 2 A.M. one summer night.
He had been dead for forty years.
He gave his grandchildren a fright.

They asked him why he had come back.
"I haven't been far off," he said.
"I never liked you much, alive,
but things are cooler now I'm dead,

greener, deeper, firmer-set
in a dimension that gives ease—
why not reach back with part of me
into time's old complexities?

For something of the all I am
was formed here, when all's said and done,
though now I walk a wider range
and scarce recall the game I won."

Enigmas

Shame

"I am two days from death
and I have no name."
What shall I call you then?
"Call me shame,
bonerack, stench and living corpse
with a hey and a ho and back to the dust."

Ugly shame,
stupid shame,
old shame two days from death!
Grin if you can
while I sing you a song
of what poor shame is worth.

Thaw

Shape a couple out of mist
or shall it be a fine hound
snowy-pale in January?

Don't expect to hunt till dawn
if no dawn is entertained
by those who are its denizens.

So dance with me, Miss Talleyrand,
in the broken-down chateau—
red berries gleam out from those vines!

In thaws of yet another March
the ice breaks, releasing death
which until now has seemed a mirror.

Aubade

Who has hold of Juliet's nipples
ramming her from behind?
Is it her very own Romeo,
or the sardonic weathered friend—
even perhaps her doddering sire
incestuously inclined?

It doesn't matter to the cat
creeping at dawn along the tiles
back to his interior self:
no thought can ambush that sly track.

The scowling cousin skulks in outer shadow.
The pumping mounts up to a brace of screams.
Old nursie in her bed turns snorting, sighing—
eases herself into commodious dreams.

Pharaoh

The Pharaoh Ikhnaton
"Living-in-Truth"
saw each thing's reality
held by the sun's rays as by hands.

Today the chill Museum shelters
what we know as "past":
residues of transient selves
rubbings of identity
a billion brittle testaments
told, effaced.

In the chance encounter
on Madison Avenue
at the fierce noon of day

Ikhnaton lives again
without his robes and jewels
without his bones and skin—

but that's forgotten, too.

Prisoner

Trapped in the house of ash
he awaited the decline of day.
Sun peaked to its zenith
above those bare peeled walls
while outer trees bowed down their latticed green.

The heat forced its extremes.
Determined to endure
he gave no smallest stir—
eye-blink nor twitch of nerve—
though all life's movements were within his compass.

The chains could not be seen.
Breathless in the parched house
choosing that house as his
he let the long day pass.
At night he would walk free among the shadows.

Mirror

The mirror turns black.
The night walks in from the sea.
There are no more faces
to watch the heron's slow flight along the shore.

Dark sand is mixed
with moistly shining stones
along the levels your naked feet once knew,

while other mirrors under sea
retain your shape implicitly
and the winds racket through the huge house and return to
  their island.

No faces any more.
Only—empty places
dark-tinctured by the sea,
awaiting those in the mirror who won't come back.

Justice

The desert is required of you,
    the waste.

Tread it or not, it will be there
    those nights
after a friend dies harshly, secretly
and from the mirror a sphinx's mask stares out.

Thoughts are sand-devils whirling
unappeased until dispersed
in as it were a leveling of
self into the process.

The Walk

for William Stafford

We walked between mountains
day by day, northward
a purple furze at our left hand
ascending white heights imperceptibly

Gradual as our walking
cold air advanced our lungs
to our right certain cliffs more sharply maintained
possibilities of sudden silence

It was a total climate
clear to the continent's end
where a few leftover Indians
were roosting in white birch tepees

and the ice, too, cracked its chasms
to blind any outreaching eye
that might beseech a black whaleboat or two
among the Eskimo inlets

The bears withdrew up into their cliffs
the seals dove under ice
the Indians slouched away whistling
and left us there with our poems

Cold Poem

Despaired of living man. Walked into a cold landscape—
all white it was—sat down there on the ground,
      froze: became man of ice.

Poor hands flapped like flags, tatters of the sky.
Built a fire to warm them, from that white wood.
      Making warmed. . . then fire warmed.

Songs returned to mind then, through pellucid air
chiming their changes from the icy Circle
      deep to heart's wolf-den.

Feeding on chill bones, teeth sparkled with mica,
gaze flared keenly over skeleton land
      ware of no second vision.

Hands led spirit forth to its exhilaration,
white column jaunting free across the ice-sheets:
      frost beglittered with fire.

Sparks flying everywhere: if one should kindle
all might be burned in the glad destruction
      and the old wager won.

Two Poems to a Dead Woman

1

Lady, the strange malignancy
which you called "love": in two more years
or three, it would have finished me.

You sought chiefly my misery
and pain, took pleasure in my tears.
Lady, you were malignancy

itself, playing your games with me,
tormenting me with guilt and fear,
twisting the love I had in me

to my own shame and injury
until I hated my young years.
This was your strange malignancy—

loathing yourself, you hated me
who would have freed you from your fears
could I have forced myself to be

the doom you sought so stubbornly!
—But I was rescued by the years
from that perverse malignancy:

they finished you, and set me free.

2

The whitish dawn had just appeared
with "rose and gold crowning her head"
when my dark soul, returned from dream,
slid through the window to my bed.
I woke. My soul seemed not my own
so mixed it was with every form
of man and woman I have known:
it lingered in that shapeless swarm.

And then I saw your shade that stood
naked and hateful in the gloom,
a beast from sleep's foul underwood
astir in the uncertain room:
the stabbing serpent-breasts outthrust,
the weasel-glitter in the eyes,
the belly-fold and wicked tuft
of jungle-black between the thighs.

What need I more of death (I thought)
who used to hold this fatal thing,
this corpse, in love's embrace? But then
the soul itself began to sing
a cool refrain of chiming verbs
austere upon the rising day—
and you, poor brute, spat out once more
your futile curse, and fled away.

The Closed House

It remained silent
                two or three centuries
windows closed,
white shutters hooked from the inside.

Outside the birds changed
                their customs, their plumage.
Certain cities dared approach—
then, withdrawing, crumbled.

Thin bands of sungleam
                flittered in those rooms.
No doubt they were the secret,
no doubt they remained

after the house sank
                one bright winter morning
down through black subsoil
under gritty tree-roots. . .

Moles delved about it,
                worms paid their visits,
still the house persisted
intact and serene

as though containing
                a large life's reflections
that moved once through those open doors
and would at leisure be resumed.

Shadows

Shadows glance the water:
down to the pool's face
the resilient light
sidles through branch-shapes.

My eyes seek their being
that merges in shade
between margins of stone,
mutable as this day.

Call it the soul, then,
bounded by rocks?
That self exists swimming.
Shadows of twigs catch at it.

A tremor, insisting
outward toward clarity
of rock-face and rim,
is the self's subtle shape.

The Gate

Hark! Hark! The watch-dogs bark—
my soul flies back into the dawn.
Through the smooth gate of ivory
false faces of this world depart,
but I pass through the gate of horn

into the veinstone of the Dream:
dense early forests under sleep
where all time's voices live as leaves
and all time's visions find their shapes
in richness of the lasting green.

Forms in the deep wood keep no name
of what they have been or will be,
but merge in dark abeyance where
the uttered Word resumes its home
in tangles of eternity. . .

I met my father walking there
gravely within the shadowed green;
he paused, and gently smiled at me
and spoke the words our years had been,
holding himself in what we were.

He spoke known things as for my good
but there was much he left unsaid
for when we parted I saw stream
from all ways of that ancient wood
shapes of the unborn, shapes of the dead—

of men and beasts and lives unknown,
serpents of gold, spirits of flame
shimmering, that swirled and blent with his
exultantly, as in a game. . .

Amid those shapes I saw my own.

Animula

"Nous nous réveillons tous au même endroit du rêve. . ."

Sleeping naked in openness
you may be bitten, raped or killed:
no telling that the god will come
or if he does, what face he'll wear.

Yet sleep—and glow, as from a crown
of innocence by which you reign
over glad summer and her games,
poor spirit stroked by mortal claws!

Sleep. And dream, if so you chance,
of time's far crossroads, knowing well
(though now in time you turn to death)
where all dreams meet you'll have your triumph.

SIX

Poems of the Two Worlds

1

The beginning is a cold wind
or the taste of mineral beneath the grass

or being lifted above the winter city
demonic in dusky air

as, to the midward of my journey,
in a February of frigid moon

the sordid clock-tower on east 94th
shone—and in Maine on the frozen point

while waves broke perishing across the rocks
breathing the icy night my heart near stopped:

and if it had, it had been as well
in the long gaze from the second world

these our deep pains are no matter—
in the night wind the stopped heart rises

rises and sings on its recovered journey
following the dark-winged intermediary

escorted by his hawks and owls:
the beginning is the cold breath

of stone and crystal at the roots—
a whisper of water from the night side—

the second world where the dead walk arm in arm,
perfected ones garbed in their destinies,

breathing their power into these airs
through the vague intervals of matter

where the circling desolate heart
awaits in turn its liberation.

2

From the Crab's whirl
            from beyond the stars
                        from blackness
a hand thrusts,
            shakes pepper from a pot:
the seeds sift through the universe in clouds,
each speck bears in itself Homunculus
crouched and scowling, thinking human thoughts. . .

The golden Egg is opening,
                        the pepper seasons it
with chance
            with abnormality of change
                        with life
that happens as it happens in its drift
as God is happening unto himself.

It all unfolds, by chance, just as it had to—
just as it must, though no one made it happen:
it comes
            departs
                        is a retaining Mind
and Not-mind, and what exceeds those both.

After breakfast, God takes his random walk
in the cool glades where nothingness has being:
his thoughts rejoin themselves beneath the trees.

3

The dark one crouching in his cave alone
withdraws strange emeralds from the sulphur spring.
The feckless gulls are morselling the ledge
above a nameless ocean's million blades.

A single sail on all that blue: it's Cook,
Bougainville or St. Brendan, or maybe
Madoc the bastard or the long-lost sire,
homing at last, of Victoria Rapahango.

Brilliant voyagers of the mind's clear stream,
sharp-featured entities with eyes of gold,
they emanate from the great throning Dream
that lurks behind this jettison of sky.

The mind dilates; contracts again, absorbs
its jewels in a deathly inner space
where yet some quick chance touch may magically
open granite doors to those bragging waves

that haunt the dark one in his reverie
with images of fate and what's beyond—
even as the gulls fly whitely forth and back
across the real and the unreal ocean. . .

The voyager still lives within the legend,
the utterer still mutely shapes the tale;
when the dark eye spies out the lonely sail
then sea-farer and cave-dweller are one

upon the bright, illimitable sphere
where shapes of life emergent from deep dream
wax, wane and blend themselves within the Change—
until the dreamer lift his changeless eye.

4

Komë Berenikes floating
        in the sea with jellyfish. . .

Rinsings of dismembered wrecks
        glimmer outside Gulnar's halls
as the drowned wights light their lamps
        phosphorescent on the rocks
where her whiskered doublemen
        display their swaying testicles.

Changelings keep the stars in mind
        each to sink his secret being
deep through the reflective dark
        where urchins vibrate in the mud
and the secular Crab awaits
        minglings of a second sun.

Stars who know their living names
        coolly urge that long awareness.
Forms within the crystal dusk
        whirl and coalesce in bliss
and lots are drawn! The worlds are one.
        Twins come now unto their own.

. . .Silent in great space the seal
        swims between the stars.

5

Pêcheur, pêcheur, avez-vous vu
la reine des ombres, la blanche Dahut?
Revisiting the Breton shore
on coal-black horse, long hair blown back,
hard on the heels of her shadow pack
she hunts the weakling dead once more.

In feeble panic see them fly,
misshapen dim nonentities
aquiver with the self's disease,
who live their lives within a lie.
The hounds' white teeth shall rend their flesh,
each coward fragment feel her lash!

Enough of that. The meaning seen
a quarter-century ago
when the dark Self put on her show
perhaps conceals what she would mean.
Let's think so, friends! whose living heads
I saw driven down among those dead.

It would appear that you are damned,
but I'll not be the one to say it.
If there's a debt, and you must pay it,
pay it you shall at her command—
proud living Bitch of my desire
from whose deep eyes my eyes take fire—

no, Heaven's not always for the meek!
But a secret's here I may not speak. . .
Past the still fisher by the stream
I thread my way through tangled paths
backwards from the place of wrath
to shallows of a nearer dream.

6

A rose dawn, in smoke, over the East River:
light is reflected from the keel of clouds
along Park Avenue's soiled streaks of snow.
My sense attends the shiftings of the cold.

Something—something reaches out behind the semblance:
dimness with claws, brutal and serene.
The sun rises across pale roofs of asphalt.
A car stops at the red on 95th, which clicks to green.

A man with a briefcase hurries to the corner,
hails a cab, speeds off in a spray of slush;
the newspaper boy in scarlet stocking cap
trundles his squeaking cart from block to block. . .

How shall I fix your shape or speak your name,
great glow-eyed Cat crouched at the roots of being?
This traffic of shadows between dark and light
obscures the pure insistence of your gaze.

And yet, extended from invisible sunlight,
it's straitly in that gaze the shadows live,
rehearse the permutations of their fates
and win such vision as may view themselves.

Somewhere, in an antiworld,
a man has risen and looks out from his window;
his face is mine, but if we should shake hands
all worlds, thoughts, gods would find their fiery end,

being reduced to your simplicity,
God, who are Any, All and None—in one.
Now, please, retire; and claws be sheathed.
Cold and bright the day's begun.

SEVEN

The Puppets

July 1973

What raised these puppets high above
    our common, struggling flesh?
Righteousness, American-style,
    well fortified by cash.

What kept them there? The shield of power
    obscuring false and true.
What dragged them out into the light?
    The courage of a few.

Why did they cheat and bite and plot
    an end to decency?
Because to puppets each true man
    is marked as enemy.

For what can things contrived of wires
    glue, plastic, styrofoam
do except hate the honest ones
    sprung still from flesh and bone?

Nerve-radiations from what brain
    waggle those legs and arms?
The programs coded in the skull
    contain their fixed alarms

until each well-groomed manikin
    turns "human" in the end
diffusing through the ambient airs
    the "person" he pretends—

of smooth-faced ad-man bright and glib,
    adept at mouthing lies—
or old false lawyer, pouchy-lipped
    with deadness in his eyes—

or crew-cut Christian Scientist
    California bred

holding the crimes of righteousness
    sealed in his bullet head. . .

But the Big Puppet, what of him
    still sitting on the wall
wearing a crown on his false head,
    who never speaks at all

except to nix the claims of truth
    by privilege of that crown:
how many repetitions, friends,
    before we pull him down?

—Dear Muse of 1973
    who see our injured state,
shore up some emblem from the past
    to signify its fate!

The blinded Belisarius
    holds in his arms his guide,
that poisoned youth whose agony
    reveals our darker road.

Five Grotesque Poems

Deborah Poem

Deborah, Deborah, where have you been?
Off to Bangkok in my flying machine.

Deborah, Deborah, what saw you there?
Serpents, pagodas, small men with no hair.

And what did you do with those elegant men?
I let them handle me now and again.

Did they love your long locks and delicate shape?
They dressed me in chains like a sacred ape.

Were you frightened? *No fear—nor any regret
that I was their darling and secret pet.*

Deborah, Deborah, what did befall?
I knew the Three Ways, and relished them all.

The Aristocrats

They sipped champagne in their chalet,
ate shellfish in a shiftless way
and shilly-shallied all the day
in shallops, on the rippling bay.

From high cold windows looking down
at night upon the huddled town
drank their liqueurs, then in deep beds
shuddered under eiderdown

dreaming of mobs that ran amok
and dragged them sniveling to the block
where soon a *chop-chop-chop* would leave
but red remains of this fair stock.

Scorning what love might understand
of life's plain passions and demands

they feared the pain of human hearts
and loathed the grit of human hands.

Limp egotists, dull snobs, poseurs,
I knew it well—that world of yours—
the heavy meals, the vacant minds,
the plays, the poodles, the chauffeurs—

Back into the mould you go!—
the destinies you would not know
fermenting blindly in the dark
where they await the next great throw.

Princess Poem

Golden eagles nip the cherries
tersely from designing branches
of those sable groves wherein
a languid princess promenades.

Who may read what thoughts drift slowly
through the placid skull that's held
firm behind her soft face-flesh
amid the gently growing gold?

Medicine was never found
could cure the clutch of mother-sickness
blazoned in the pumpkin king's
ruddy gape of aching laughter—

Heliodora! Your svelte semblance
hangs within my stony chamber
mirror-sharp, beside the stuffed
penis of a bull-baboon

while the ashy pikemen lead
father-king to a high scaffold
where amid the winds and crows
a certain head will tumble down.

Underwings of silky birdlets
glimmer thinly from the copse
as princess, all brocades unclenched,
slumps naked to the moony lawn.

The Remnant

Totem-pole man looks in my window
fat hooked beak and goggling eyes
Totem-pole man says *Big wind coming*
run to the mountain quick and hide

Clutch my wife and call my children
Drop your toys don't say goodbye
quick as cats we run to the mountain
crawl in a cave and build a fire

Big wind comes, blows down the city
ocean waters drown the roofs
damned ones howl, float on their bellies
Saved we chew on grains and roots

Waters ebb wind falls to whisper
birds streak sky with ashy gleams
Speechlessly we stride back homeward
through fresh marshes, swollen streams

Something looms across the mudflats
Totem-pole man tall as a cloud!
Scarlet cheeks glow, black beak opens
Heard my word, myself am god.

The Further Adventures of

Too many cars in Manhattan tonight.
Creep out with blow-gun and darts.
Pierce the sick spooks through their eyeballs.
They'll be dead before even they smash.

Slyly then slip around corners and down
West Street by the misty docks.
Climb rotting stairs to the stink-hole
where the hag, the foul lover, awaits.

Black tusks the better to chomp you old boy,
a mug all craters and scabs!
Hunching the floor like an orang
she slobbers her vile hexacola.

Bolt the door. Speak her name in a whisper.
Rising, she drops the sour smock
stained stiff with her spittle and shit
and lets loose a long welcoming howl—

standing naked once more as blonde girl-child
cool by the reticent bulb
while ancient freighters departing
groan out their farewells from the harbor.

Five Ballets

Elves

The notion of living entities in human shape, intelligent but not human: look upon it as an experiment conducted upon the stuff of being. Shall they be smaller than we? Bushier, perhaps? What impulses bring about these particular condensations? To what extent do the alien existences depend upon certain crystallizations of our own thought, perhaps upon our very words? Shall we postulate *elves*, speaking the word aloud so as to give life to a certain meaningful vibration? But then we have become responsible for them and must find them a bodily home. Is the preference for frail and exquisite manikins? Or elongated, wispy personages clad in forest green? Or small fat burly chaps with beards? "The elves hold their revels," I say. "They revel on the meadows in the moonlight." The stage is set; the action begins. Little whiskery creatures cavort in the pale gloam, guzzle beer from oaken kegs, kick off their britches and fart, and let their balls swing in the midnight breezes. These elves are from a vulgar tradition, which I happen to like.

"Eleven elves reveled on the level velvet veldt." I summoned them long ago: their existence is not in question. Secure in their borderland homes, they inhabit a climate well adjusted to their several moods, and maintain a well-recognized pattern of activity—which is, to be sure, somewhat circumscribed and ritualistic. But there is a twelfth elf, a doubting Thomas, who observes them as they fulfill their moonlit rounds but himself neither moves nor speaks.

I go out by night and watch them occasionally, under a sky of indigo.

Demons

We must circumscribe these strong personalities, or they will overcome us.

I have banished them, tentatively, to the depths of an imaginary Pleistocene, amidst monster saurians and tetrapods, in a landscape where the rule "Eat or be eaten" is somewhat unimaginatively observed. Here they live in interlinked caverns reaching back endlessly from the face of a black, titanic cliff. They are furred in black, with white fangs and eyes that spark red like coals. Almost all have tails—long, feline, prehensile—and occasionally one will develop a pair of leathery retractable wings, though these are fortunately seldom adequate for flight. The nipples of the females emerge—blue or violet—from a modest moss of black; the lips of their genitalia, seldom seen, are somewhat enlarged and of a startling scarlet. The males are larger and shaggier, more truculent in attitude: when one is aroused, his eyes dilate and his penis, long and flexible as a tail, extends itself down to his ankles. They bellow or howl at times, but seldom fight, as they know their power is being reserved for other occasions. In copulation, the penis— moving independently but supple as a snake—enters the soft labia slowly and hesitantly, while the tails, in convulsive gropings, intertwine.

Black figures emerge from the cave-mouths and move about the cliff-face, using hands, feet, tails, to ascend and descend. They scour the swamp and jungle in packs, crushing between their teeth the strong leathery insects, swallowing serpents whole, tearing large mammals apart limb from bleeding limb. So they eat—and are themselves sometimes eaten by larger, more mindless brutes.

In the innermost cave, where they sometimes congregate, an image of the earth is hung. They point to it, gesticulating eagerly. Some have already returned; the others are waiting to follow—when the sacred moment arrives.

Angels

The clouds of childhood seem endlessly white: they contain in their intricate reaches a vast collection of countries, of continents—discrete, irresponsible, aglow, like gems strung on an endless chain.

Angels who personify the imaginings of children preside over these realms. They too are of an apparently enduring whiteness. They may take the guise of small puffy clouds, of sheep, of large birds—or, at night, of comets conceived as womanlike with streaming hair.

Blessings here, and threatenings—but only in sketchwork of potency. Images are not yet fully expressed nor meanings formulated. There may well be beaches of Aegean purity, bordered in cypress, washed by pale waves: but any temple found nestling on those shores must be vacant. You may encounter secret trails of blood, heaps of excrement bleaching in the sun; but the band of poetical redskins that comes shrieking to your summons has only a provisional reality.

Countries of long grasses, yes, where intelligent horses roam and graze, giving expression to a purely animal freedom; countries of sand and rock, where the bones of all once living things foregather, conversing of those matters dreamed to be *essential;* countries all forest and fruit, inhabited only by dragonflies and birds—and the birds of so many colors that even the faceted eyes of the dragonflies cannot distinguish them all.

Such lands, then, exist? No. But in some sense reality may be reflected in these fragments that are so beautiful, inept, and incommunicado. And I myself have visited at least one. Those gardens, stretching endlessly before me in the finest of mists, beneath an unchanging sky of first dawn, where before me down the paths of white gravel no one had walked but the single gardener—surely it was an angel who brought me there, momentarily, one early morning forty years ago! (And before I departed, I saw the gardens of women, naked in harness of pure amethyst.)

These early angels are always at play; they roll their dice from cups of carved black jade. And themselves take on the being of the coded cubes, glinting in their finite permutations. They lounge, they chatter—they adopt for themselves secret Pythagorean names: Oregano, Apteryx, Aldebaran, Sharmuz, Kraken, Wendigo . . . They love mathematics, puzzles, games. They fear the human body.

But those others, bearers of the shapes of our destinies, vivid as jets of sperm, as gashings of stars, when will they arrive with their desperate human faces? We must await the toss of the unmarked dice, from the cup of bottomless night.

Pterodactyls

I have always regarded them as friends. Somewhat grotesque, but dutiful in their comings and goings, and forming a necessary link in the chain of existence. I was therefore displeased, at age thirteen, to see one crumpled between the paws of a hulking apish brute and tossed to the waves below as if he were no more than the flimsy wreckage of an archaic and defective aeroplane. There was a structure here that merited more consideration.

It is true that one will occasionally, flying through an open window at night, seize a sleeping girl—naked or in filmy nightdress—and abscond with her to some distant mountain or inaccessible rooftop. But her fate is not desperate. He will usually bring her directly back to her own room and bed—after having set her down in that lonely place, stalked about her three or four times in awkward circles, and given her the once-over with his unblinking quizzical gaze. (Perhaps even, with his long bony beak, pecked gently once or twice at her nipples or belly button.)

Counterbalancing this foolishness, one must insist on their usefulness as messengers. Featherless birds, hovering between the serpent and the angel, they possess an intelligence which is more than vestigial but limits itself to immediate practicalities. Their lack of imagination is refreshing: without drama or self-aggrandizement they may bring tidings from above or below. When one of them comes looming down and settles himself before you, creaking and flapping—then takes an ungainly step and, cocking his ugly head, looks squarely into your eyes—you will know he brings a message that had best be heeded.

Nightwatchers

for Paula

We hear them at dawn, a small golden ringing that comes
from many leagues off, distorted by distance. . . Or from
the innermost coilings of our own ears. . . And laughter,
that begins and ends with the sound of wind passing
through leafy branches. Were they in our rooms watching
us while we slept? Or amusing themselves in the moonlight
of our quiet furniture?

Mysterious ringings and tinklings! Do they have bells,
musical instruments? Or do they summon up these sounds
from powers that rest within ourselves? It is, in any case, a
music to which no meaning may be assigned.

Yet it tempts us, with a suggestion of departures. From
our silent rooms, in which (if we could but observe them at
a time when they are totally unobserved) a faint track of
motion might perhaps be detected; from our sleeping bod-
ies (are we inside or outside them when they sleep?), out of
whose webwork entire creations have risen into being; and
from the specified, given world—as when someone steps
away from a mirror and his reflection disappears.

We think of them as of a multiplicity of individual enti-
ties, in communication with one another, each one perhaps
searching our world for his mortal twin. At dawn, as our
windows grow palely bright and bodies recover the aware-
ness of self, they withdraw into the eternal forest: where
they dream of us, as we—sometimes—of them.

EIGHT

Saying

There always is another way to say it.

As when you come to a dusty hill and say,
"*This* is not the hill I meant to climb.
That one I've perhaps climbed already—see,
there it looms, behind me, green with trees."
And then climb as you can the present hill.

Or when you walk through a great childhood forest
latticed with sun, carpeted in brown pine,
knowing the one you were and the one you are,
and think, "I shall not speak this forest's name
but let it densely live in what I am. . ."

The saying changes what you have to say
so that it all must be begun again
in newer reconcilings of the heart.

Being, I

God
sitting at midday outside the cafe at Aix
where it had brightened after quick-scattering showers,
sitting with a half-empty glass just taking his time
(you didn't see him come, won't notice when he leaves)

or on a fine spring afternoon in New York
stepping out upon a never-used balcony
overlooking Madison, enjoying the hot sun
and the stink of traffic, biding there a while
before turning back inside where no one will know

or watching the olive girls play tag at evening
in Rio, in the Jardim Botanico
pausing in the long aisle of elegant palms
to enjoy the dancing breasts and gleaming eyes
while high in the dusk one star begins its gleaming—

he always seems to be making the best of things,
pleasantly unconcerned. . . but you're never sure
what is his real being, what his "mere appearance"
or whether it matters. How can you tell, after all,
since he may be "infinity" or just a wisp of cloud?

The realization is somehow in *you*. Because, of course,
there's no meaning in his great Name: it's all in the
glimpse.

Music

(from the Han Fei Tzu)

In ancient times
the Yellow Emperor
assembled the spirits at the summit of Mount T'ai.
It was in Autumn, when the dying begins.

Tigers and wolves in his vanguard
ghosts and elementals roaming behind
he rode in an ivory carriage, drawn
by six slouched dragons.
Overhead, through the chill sky, phoenixes soared.

The Wind Lord cleared his passage
the Rain Master sprinkled his road
and a god kept pace with the linchpin,
a god whose name was not known.

Standing, then, at the cold peak
amid thin swirls of cloud
he called the beings together
from all the realms and quarters

and with them, created music:
those austere intervals of the *chüeh* mode,
the saddest and the purest.

"In a five-minute stillness in September"

In a five-minute stillness in September
the sunlight not yet departing from the goldenrod
that straggled down to shore's edge

it seemed all at once as if all might be understood—
if not articulately, at least in depth of heart—
by some less developed life-form,

some being that would move, eat, procreate and so on
but without the cutting edge of arrogance
that so disfigures our kind,

whose brain, pale instrument too fine for its data,
will, left to itself with nothing better to do,
multiply small distinctions

endlessly, uselessly in a tight compulsion
to impose its structure on the stuff of existence—
which indeed will bend itself

but only up to a certain unassayable point
beyond which, if the mind wander, it wanders untethered
from the glad solemn animal

holding to the heart of time, and holding in its own heart
as fulfillment of joy and pain (on days of September sun)
the certitude of being.

From the I Ching

Heaven—encircling—is ruler and father,
metal, jade, ice, the tinge of deep red,
a strong horse, an old horse, a lank horse and piebald,
the fruit of the fruit-tree, the sun on the hill.

Earth is the mother: thrift and stability,
fibers, fabrics, a caldron, vast throngs,
a handle, a heifer, a large open carriage,
the shade in the valley, the taste of black soil.

Moment

for Paula

Behind the Elizabeth Perkins House at York
marigolds glow against a weathered fence.
Bright chilly air of an October morning:
we hold life cleanly at our fingertips.

"I love grim Autumn days"

I love grim Autumn days,
leaves falling yellow, brown
into the rainy gutters
along Fifth Avenue.

Life not so freely given
as in glad summertime
but durably maintained:
thus has my life found meaning.

Things yield their uttermost
only in death's conjunction—
I need not tell you this,
dear Paula, you who held
your dying brother's head.

Recall the legend, how
washed up by a murdering ocean
the princess found in white sand
a simple golden key,
the only one that might unlock
dungeons she was yet to come upon. . .

The answer we are given, then,
precedes the possible questions
as the moment, all of gold,
precedes time's reach before and after—
and death, too, is there with its meaning
before a life begins.

Now the season speaks
at once of death and harvest—
of time that seeks fulfillment
as, love, you release the moments
locked in autumnal faces.

Walking the streets at duskfall
to a room that may become timeless

we think of lovers set free
to step forth into their legends:

and, at last, our own dying bodies
shall clasp in the joyous moment
while outside our still windows
the darkness settles down.

The Depths

Watered light of winter:
rain, sleet on the city.
No need to speak, we are hand in hand
walking undersea blocks
to the room we know that knows us.

The bed may be from Manaos
(rosewood spirals dull-gleaming):
it knows our bodies once more, while ourselves
find one another new-fledged
this day as our sun thrusts down
through canopy of trees in Brazil
to glint on a pool's dark surface.

Might it pierce, even, the great outer
ocean, tinting those halls
where the old lords and ladies still dance?
Their measures extend beyond time
as we ourselves yield to a rhythm
that reaches, now, more searchingly down.
Listen. We rise in the stillness

and stand hand in hand by the window
gazing at roofs in the mist.
Dear companion, we're up from the depths!
—joy hidden bright in our mouths,
each holding the taste of the other.

Winter Poem

for Paula

We made love on a winter afternoon
and when we woke, hours had turned and changed,
the moon was shining, and the earth was new.
The city, with its lines and squares, was gone:
our room had placed itself on a small hill
surrounded by dark woods frosted in snow
and meadows where the flawless drifts lay deep.
No men there—some small animals all fur
stared gently at us with soft-shining eyes
as we stared back through the chill frosty panes.
Absolute cold gave us our warmth that night,
we held hands in the pure throes of delight,
the air we breathed was washed clean by the snow.

Lao-Tzu

Lao-Tzu is walking still among the evergreens
bearded and bushy-browed,
his fifteen-hundred-year-old stag behind him:
he bids you cease your pitiful contentions,
live with restraint, cherish the growth of things
and die in time as women and men.

After a Painting by Buson

One sweep of your broom
old scrubber, old mother,
and the earth is clean gone.

A Forgotten Poem

I lost it this morning
in a cloud of enlightenment:
God—it's yours.

"The devil demands perfection"

The devil demands perfection
　　　　so that he may annul it
through our own apprehension
　　　　of all those dread tomorrows.

Perfection implies striving
　　　　onward, day by day.
Better to move than arrive—
　　　　so runs the old cliché—

and Satan likes his motion!
　　　　Outward from what he is
in nervous orbitings
　　　　that dissipate his being.

His claws kept Faust agog.
　　　　He's got them in us now,
twitching about "at the threshold
　　　　of the computer age."

This massed stupidity
　　　　fell long ago from heaven
thinking itself no doubt
　　　　spectacularly tragic.

A star! a star! we seek
　　　　guaranteed brave arrivals,
blind to what may already
　　　　(where we are) be shining,

what lost and tranquil planet
　　　　bathed in the Self's still rays—
no light of "man's perfection"
　　　　lengthens those perfect days. . .

But who will mind such presence
　　　　now the Space Age has begun

with its gift of endless flight-plans
        from sun to trivial sun

and its promises of perfection
        just beyond our grasp
that will keep the anxious brain-cells
        fidgeting to the last. . .

Can man outgrow his future,
        let be that sham of stars?
The devil demands perfection—
        but God takes what we are.

"Anger at my heart one April morning"

Anger at my heart one April morning
and before St. Vincent Ferrer's the tulip trees in bloom. . .

You wrestle with yourself as with an angel
who leaves you maimed and scarred. Let him prevail,
he'll weigh you down into nonentity,
but if you win, it's only for the day:
he's always back to try you out again.

I saw my fellow once, up in the sky
riding a cloud above the Chrysler Building
whose spire gleamed in gold—but what his face looks like
I haven't known, for always in our struggles
he keeps his head turned downward and away.

At the circus a few days ago a clown
fell from a high wire into the lions' cage
which—for publicity—served as a net.
The creatures roared, showed anger, but the tamer
held them at bay while the hurt clown rolled free.
He's in the hospital now, recovering;
soon will be fit to do his act again.

Admirable, to define yourself this way?
Yes, partly, for the courage and persistence.
But what's the final sense, if you know you yearn
to be at one with the prime animal
who'd clasp you to him in his raging love—
the six-winged beast all circleted with eyes?

You try to talk to God, to come to terms.
Not easy—particularly if that self
you see as you, is grasped too definitely.
Too easy then to start the act all over,
God fading into a sort of wishfulness—
but let that sense of self blur a bit, grow vague,
you'll slip through these big temporary meshes

and find yourself. Where? In the world where all is known.
For suddenly the wrestlers disengage,
each seeing the angel in the other's eye—
the angel who, in each, is the same "I"—
and all is stilled within the sun's great blaze.

The passions then, released, ride the high winds
and God himself roars with them and rejoices.

Umbrella Poem

Old pale lady walking in the rain
                    beneath her green umbrella:
face webbed with lines, somewhat tired,
eyes peering out from a powdery surface—
frailness,
                    but asserting its own direction!

Within the gray-white 5 P.M. light
she advances her own small circle of green
that becomes (for me) the signet of spring
as beyond her I see Park Avenue's islands
drenched and glowing in their deeper green.

May 1, 1974

for Paula

Through slats of our half-open shutters
I see green branches stirring
of lindens in hot sun
in the courtyard of St. Sergius' across the street.

Here in the blue studio
that strong light is subdued
as it angles in through the slats and across the bookshelves.
I have opened one window
and sit here in my usual chair
while sounds of spring come freely in from the street:
the screams of children playing ball
clop of ball on pavement
calls, complaints of mothers
squeak of delivery-bikes
bellowing of the old concierge at the Rumanian Embassy
who directs the parking of cars—
behind it all, the hustle of traffic going up and down Park.

Our indoor colors are rich in the afternoon glow.
On the chest your red-framed Picasso poster lies
waiting until we find the right precise spot for it.
Over the mantel Duke William's tapestry hangs tawny-bright.

I am thinking of a poem.
I am thinking also of making love to you
on our Portuguese bed, the moment you arrive.
Meanwhile, someone downstairs has begun cooking supper
    early
and even as I write, the light grows subtly cooler.

—It was not long ago—two weeks or a little more—
that on a chilly midnight
we awaited on this street
the procession to the Tomb:
those ancient bearded priests, those crucifers icons and
    banners

rounding the corner of the house built by the Chairman of the
   New York Central
passing through the court and up the outside stairs to the
   ballroom
which is now their chapel
and also, for one moment each year, the Tomb of Christ.
The knocking at the gate then. Empty! "He is risen."
The bearded one turns about in his blessed amazement
("Christos Basileus—Christ the King is risen!"
Defective loudspeakers gargle in Slavic gutturals)
and blesses us below.
The faithful cross themselves,
the cheap frame of light bulbs tacked up over the courtyard
flares out the miracle: X B

Easter. Faithful and faithless
we light our candles, we of the throng—
one by one, each from his neighbor—
to be held in one hand a few moments, the fire guarded in the
   curve of the other,
while the procession enters rejoicing
the Tomb that has opened, now, to a peopled heaven
where soon the chanting will begin.

I, as always,
take my flame from yours.

Autobiographies

1

I lay on my back in Portugal
the storks were flying over
   white green white
on their way from the Coto Doñana
   white white blue
numina enskied:

I watched them through the fingers of one hand.

2

I am up at five, have coffee, read my paper on the terrace—
at eight, close shutters and blinds: the rooms are sealed.
In a morning twilight (one window alone half open)
I do some writing at the cardinal's desk
then go out, take care of my errands and pay a few calls.
I like to get my work done before noon—

Have lunch at one, make love, and sleep till four
while down in the piazza the workmen are asleep
lying, their heads on their arms, full length on the pavement
and the little boys curl up in the shade of the columns.
The city sounds are muted; the air is still.
This is the quietest time.
                 Soon after four
the seabreeze comes in and life begins again.
Tea on the terrace: the streets are filled with people.
The girls, always so charming, are wearing pink muslin this
   year
and dinner seems to be pushed back later and later.
We seldom dine alone. It's a time for friends,
for candlelight—
cold chicken, a light white wine, fresh fruit and ices. . .

At night we sit out in the coolness, under stars.

3

I found the place at last—
twenty-five miles due west
of the humid capital:
an inconspicuous cluster of huts
in a small jungle clearing.
A brown man in fatigues
was patrolling, carbine ready.
Insects hummed.
I climbed into the branches
of a low tree, and waited.

Just after dark a storm broke—
solid rain like a lake overturned
flare after flare of sheet lightning—
I hunched, shifted my grip
and heard soon, under the thunder,
a dull groaning and clanking.
Trucks creeping down the rutted path
broke into the clearing—four of them.
They stopped, men jumped down,
others ran out from the huts
and after some shouting in Spanish
began the unloading.
I could see, by the intermittent glare,
the long thin crates that held the guns.

Two nights later at the waterfront bar
the strip-teaser, to finish off her act,
thrashing naked on her back on the narrow stage
spread her thighs screaming and inserted a banana—
to the huge approval of the military.

4

Arrived at the foot of the Maiden:
glaciers, torrents
nine hundred feet in visible descent
and minute by minute avalanches falling
like thunder.
                    I gathered snow there,
crushed it to hardness in my hands
while sound of cowbells
rose from the remote pastures.
Saw no man. The air, distilled,
was sharper than on a January day at home.

And then the storm came on—
hail, thunder, lightning, all in their perfection
beautiful as the last day of the Eon,
the day of finished things.
I thought of other lives,
shaped sternly as my own—
subtle, austere, each imbued with its own finality.
Looked up through the hail:
the torrent's shape was curved over the rock
not mist nor water but something in between,
tail of a white horse streaming in the wind.

5

A narrow room with rush blinds
straw carpet
a table and mat—
the mind being calm and at ease
simple beauties gratify the eye
—as, behind the house, a grassy slope that goes down to the
     river—
and common daily sounds delight the ear.

123

To hold to the simple present.
A meal of vegetables,
soup of boiled greens, will do:
the mind, cleared of sediment,
resting on its emptiness
mastering the great principle—
shoes of coarse hemp
robes of coarse cloth
granting body such ease as it requires
until its day of death.

From the Kuan-Tzu

East is the time of stars:
its country is the spring.
Winds yield wood and bone
growth, abundance, joy.
Make clean the spirit's places
set house and land in order
plant, cultivate the fields
repair bridges and dams.
Pardon all who have wronged you
make compromises, adjustments
send gifts to those you love
be open in all directions.
Then shall the slow rains fall
and winds blow softly their promise
of calm lives attaining ripe age,
of animals waxing and thriving.

South is the time of the sun:
its land is the land of summer.
Fire shapes pure act
rejoicing in its sufficiency
consumed in very being
as free gift and enjoyment.
Pause then, take your pleasure
in the self's proud assertion
life's long-stayed fruitions
love and love's diversions.

West is the time of the zodiac:
its country is the autumn.
Metal deep in earth
sends forth its glint of sadness
nails and horns and antlers
severity and silence.
Search yourself within
keen-set against all laxness,

dare not be dissolute
strictly seek uprightness.

North is the time of the moon:
its country is the winter.
Water inures to ice,
snow scatters on meadow,
cold nourishes rich blood
with flares of mild anger.
Hope scatters in darkness
but blood moves powerfully:
seek purity within
store up in secrecy.

At center stands the earth:
its country is for ever.
It gives each season in turn
the strength that makes it stable.
Friend of the wind and rain
impartial, correct
it builds the flesh of bodies
and gives this breathing world
harmony and poise
from which to live the changes.

Mary

After Jesus died and was buried, the rumors
began to spread of various manifestations:
a page was turned, a new strange chapter begun.
Mary, however, spent most of her time at home

quietly living her life out. Certain things
remembered or discovered, which she had set
long ago in her heart, commanded her still.
Her life only was hers, after all. She knew it.

And so, when important persons came to call
asking her questions about her son—Who was he?
What had he claimed to be?—she only smiled
and gave no answer. They went off displeased,

but she knew very well there were no words
for her to utter. She could only be—
as pledge of truth that dwells beneath all words
and lives on darkly flowing, like a stream.

The years passed. She was more and more herself:
gentler, sterner to the end. No need
to call that fragile body up to heaven
who knew her heaven within, and died content.

The Step

From where you are at any moment you
may step off into death.
Is it not a clinching thought?
I do not mean a stoical bravado
of making the great decision blade in hand
but the awareness, all so simple, that
right in the middle of the day
you may be called to an adjoining room.

Prayer

God, who are strange to me,
I thank you for the years
stranging me from a self
I may no longer be.

That creature of one time—
anguished, young, perplexed—
I find him still in me
but am no longer he,

for selves fade into Self
as the years turn and change,
and strangeness becomes home
where nothing can be strange.

Being, II

God always was
but never knew his meaning
until he had creation
to see in, as a mirror.

Felt the stain of suffering
in share of the world's being—
then, a shock of freedom
opening to his joy.

For one swerve of sameness
was stranger to himself there
coming to new seeing
as of a huger sphere

that was his own dear body
pure, impure together,
juncture of his dreams
and sacred wastes beyond.

Question

If you were pure as you wish to be
would you write the poems you want—
the ones whose beauty dazzles you from your innards?

Perhaps so, up to the point
where the balance subtly shifts
and you are purer than you knew you wished.

The poems, then, may hesitate
almost as though unavailing
against a presence that is so simply there

and, finally, dissipate
within the large contentment
of knowing that their being has been known.

Poetry from Illinois

History Is Your Own Heartbeat
Michael S. Harper (1971)

The Foreclosure
Richard Emil Braun (1972)

The Scrawny Sonnets and Other Narratives
Robert Bagg (1973)

The Creation Frame
Phyllis Thompson (1973)

To All Appearances: Poems New and Selected
Josephine Miles (1974)

Nightmare Begins Responsibility
Michael S. Harper (1975)

The Black Hawk Songs
Michael Borich (1975)

The Wichita Poems
Michael Van Walleghen (1975)

Cumberland Station
Dave Smith (1976)

Tracking
Virginia R. Terris (1976)

Poems of the Two Worlds
Frederick Morgan (1977)